Options Trading For Beginners:

Tips, Formulas and Strategies For Traders to Make Money with Options

By

Dale Blake

Table of Contents

Introduction 5

Chapter 1. Basics of Trading Options 7

Chapter 2. Options Strategies 13

Chapter 4. Tips for Successful Options Trading 27

Chapter 5. Risk Management Tips for Option Traders 32

Conclusion 33

Thank You Page 34

Options Trading For Beginners: Tips, Formulas and Strategies For Traders to Make Money with Options

By Dale Blake

© Copyright 2015 Dale Blake

Reproduction or translation of any part of this work beyond that permitted by section 107 or 108 of the 1976 United States Copyright Act without permission of the copyright owner is unlawful. Requests for permission or further information should be addressed to the author.

This publication is designed to provide accurate and authoritative information in regard to the subject matter covered. This work is sold with the understanding that the publisher is not engaged in rendering legal, accounting, or other professional services. If legal advice or other expert assistance is required, the services of a competent professional person should be sought.

First Published, 2015

Printed in the United States of America

Introduction

You must have seen it on television commercials or full page adverts in newspapers and journals or have been emailed by someone regarding "get rich quick" promises. All one is required is to have some stated amount of dollars and attend some conference. Rub off this notion since it is not the best way to learn about the benefits of trading in options. Options trading is a difficult subject when compared with other forms of investment, for instance stocks. Therefore, many people shy away from getting into options trading. However, there is a good number of potential investors who need to acquire more information before getting involved in trading options. In their learning, however, sheer determination and effort is paramount and will determine one's success in the long run.

Although the subject is difficult to learn, nothing is too complex to an extent that its basics cannot be understood. Learning about the basics of options provides a base for further grip on deeper aspects of what actually takes place and that will eventually make sense. Trading in options allows the investor to reduce risk and have an improved chance of a gain in the stock market. However, it is essential to understand the operation of options before investing in them.

Chapter 1. Basics of Trading Options

What is an Option?

After a bit of introduction to options, you mind may be ringing questions like, what are options and why would someone invest in them?

An option is a binding contract to buy or sell a distinct financial instrument usually referred to as option's underlying interest. It is a precise contract and is established at particular price at which an agreement is arrived. This price is called the strike price. Besides, an option is time bound and has an expiry date. Beyond this date, the contract ceases to exist.

Options are of two types namely; calls or puts with both types having the ability to be sold or bought. Regarding this, you can choose to buy or sell or choose a call or put depending on your goals as an investor. For instance, in a scenario where one buys a call option, then he has the right but with no obligation to purchase a stock at the strike price before the expiry date of the option. The same applies to buying a put option where you acquire right minus obligation to sell a stock at the agreed price before the expiry of the period of investment.

To heighten the understanding about options, it is significant to differentiate it with stocks. The primary difference however, is that stocks gives you a small ownership of the company while options are binding contracts that gives you the right to sell or buy the stock at an agreed strike price within specified dates. Since it involves either buying or selling, two parties are involved.

What is a Call Option?

This is the option to buy the underlying stock at an agreed price (strike price) before a predetermined date (expiry date). The buyer of the call holds the right to purchase the stock within this period while the seller ("writer") has the obligation. If the call buyer makes a decision to buy the option (exercising the option) then the seller is expected to sell the stock to the call buyer at the strike price.

An example on this will deepen the grip. Say, a trader bought a call option at a certain company at $40 expiring in three months. The call buyer possesses the right to exercise that option paying the agreed strike price of $40 per share and receiving the shares. The call seller has an obligation of transferring the ownership of the shares and should be contented with the $40 he/she is receiving.

What is a Put Option?

Having known more about a call, one can unsurprisingly predict correctly what a put option is. This is the agreement between two parties where one has the right to sell the other at a predetermined strike price shares and the other party is obliged to buy them at that price.

Consider a case where investors bought shares of a company that has been financially healthy in the past two years. They believe that the company might continue doing well but perhaps in the verge of economic slowdown and might soon decline in the market thus they buy put option at a strike price of $50 to protect their gains. Here, buyers of the put option possess the right to sell their stock at $50 until the expiry date. The sellers of the put are obliged to purchase the shares at the agreed price of $50 which could hurt should there have been a decline in the price beyond this price.

Why are Options Relevant?

One may not see the sense brought about by the content already discussed. Well, this is a profit making business for instance; a call buyer would hope that the prices of the stock invested would rise so that he/she makes a profit. The call writer on the opposite side hopes that the share price declines such that it should be at least less than the amount received when entering the contract.

Similarly, the put buyer gains when the share price declines. A put rises in value when the initial stock price falls. Conversely, the writer of a put hopes for the option to expire with the share price above the strike price or an allowance for the stock to decline only up to the amount they gained from selling the put.

From the above therefore, we realize that options are tradable securities and can lead to profit and loss. There are many benefits on trading in options such as:

1. Options traders can profit in flat markets.

2. Options act as cover or insurance to invested stock that is unstable by pooling of risks.

3. Trading in options can triple your money overnight.

4. They can also be used to source steady flow of income from portfolios of blue chip stocks.

What is a Premium?

When you buy an option, the price incurred is called a premium. If you sell, the amount received is also referred to a premium. This premium is not fixed and changes with time. This implies that the premium you pay or receive today will not be necessarily the same as that which will be paid or received for the same options tomorrow. This price is reached by an agreement between the seller and the buyer.

Volatility

This is the tendency of the price of the tradable securities to fluctuate either to rise or fall. It portrays the extent of price fluctuation rather than the direction of the movement of the price. Therefore, premiums play a great role in the volatility of prices of options. Thus, the more volatile the underlying stock may be imply a higher premium. A general statement will therefore suggest that volatile stocks attract higher premiums for both calls and puts with the reverse being true.

Chapter 2. Options Strategies

Having introduced the two types of options which are calls and puts; it has been illustrated that there are two sides to an option transaction which are the buyer and the seller. We have discussed how volatile the prices may be and how they are set. Options strategies implies tying concepts that affect price of the stock together in a graph of profit and losses.

The strategies can be best defined by an illustration using a graph at the option's expiry date. The x-axis is used to show the price level of an option. On the other hand the y-axis represents the gain (above the x-axis) or loss (below the x-axis). Each graph will also be having its break-even point labeled for the strategy being highlighted. The graphs are meant to provide more understanding on the subject.

a. Long Call Strategy

This is the most popular strategy with investors since listed options came into the market. Before one ventures into more complicated strategies, it is paramount that one learns the fundamentals about buying and holding options. This strategy suits best to an investor whose concern is the dollar amount of his initial outlay and the reward in terms of leveraged finance that long calls can offer. The investor's push on this strategy is to achieve a financial gain due to a rise in the underlying securities. To select the right option at the right price and expiry date; one needs to have experience and precision. The diagram below illustrates the long call option strategy.

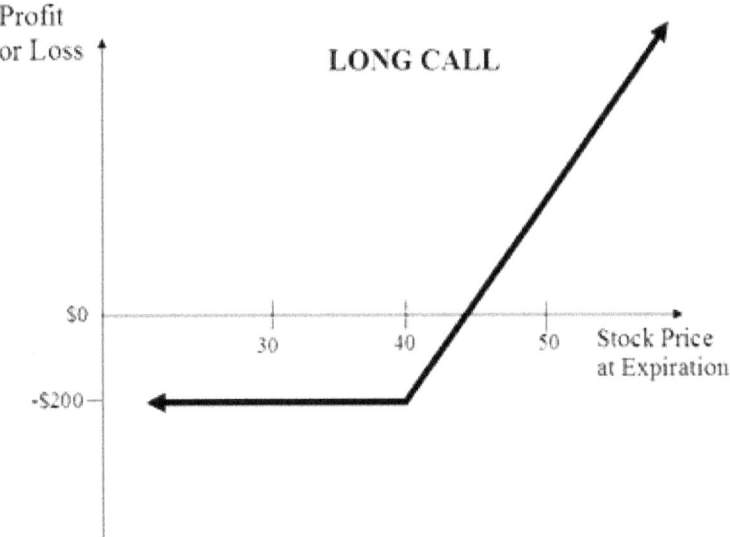

A call buyer instead of buying the underlying stock prefers the lower dollar cost of buying a call contract to an equal value of stock as form of a cover. The capital that is unused is "insured" against a drop in the price of the call option's underlying stock, and may be ploughed back elsewhere. The investor here is more concerned about the number of shares underlying the call contracts bought than the amount of the initial outlay. While holding the call option, the options trader possesses the right to purchase the same quantity of shares at the predetermined strike price before the expiry of the contract.

Long calls benefit the investor by providing leveraged alternative to a position in the stock. As the gains from the contract increase, leverage can lead to enormous profits because buying calls needs lower up-front commitment of capital than an outright buying of the underlying stock.

This strategy is meant to shed some light on options trading. This is the simplest of all and is the most common type of strategy so that once you have mastered it, you can confidently try on more intricate strategies later on.

Potential Profit

Since the asset price may rise to any level at expiration, then there is no limit to the profit attainable when trading long call options strategy.

Potential Loss

When trading long call options the risk involved is reduced to the price paid for the call option regardless of how low the asset price is trading on the date of expiry.

Break-even Point

In options trade, the most significant part is the break-even point; you should establish the break-even point long before you invest your money. The formula highlighted below is used to establish the break-even point.

Break-even point = Premium paid + Strike price of the long call.

b. Long Put Strategy

This strategy operates directly on the opposite of long call options strategy. It involves the trader buying put options with the forecast that the price of the underlying asset will decline beyond the strike price before the expiry of the period of investment. The diagram below illustrates how the strategy operates.

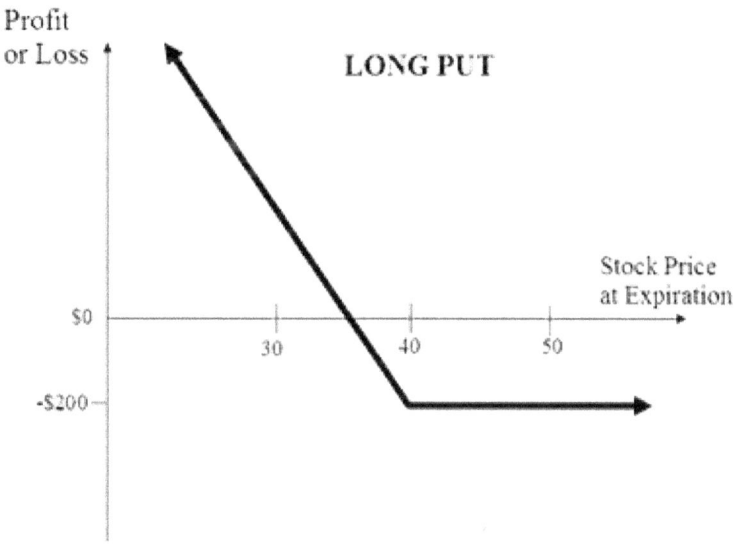

Are Put Options Similar to Short Selling?

Buying of puts can be compared to short selling though there are basic merits of buying puts instead of short selling stock. For example, it's better to bet against a stock by buying put options as you don't have to leverage the stock to short. Besides, the risk is capped to the premium paid, as opposed to the adverse risk when short selling the asset outright. However, the disadvantage is, put options have limited lifespan. If the underlying asset does not fall beyond the strike price before the option expires, the option will expire worthless.

Profit Potential

Since the asset price can nullify at expiration, the maximum profit achievable in the long put strategy is reduced to the strike price of the purchased put minus the price incurred for the option. A simple algorithm that can be used to calculate the profit potential for any given long put option.

Profit gained when price of underlying asset is zero= Strike price of long put option-Premium incurred

Since the price of the asset can get to zero at its expiry date, then maximum profit can be attained.

Potential Loss

There is a risk of implementing the long put strategy that is geared to the price paid for the put option regardless of how high the asset price may be at the expiry date.

Break-even Point

The price that is underlying at which the long put position breaks even can be calculated as shown below.

Break-even point = Strike Price of the Long Put − Premium Paid.

c. Covered Calls Strategy

This is an advanced options strategy that involves writing one call option for every a hundred shares you hold in the underlying assets. The diagram below illustrates how it works.

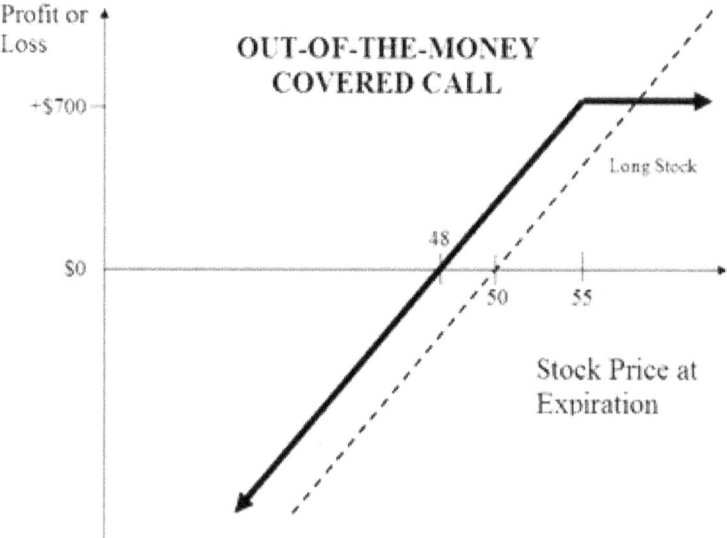

By using the covered calls strategy, you earn a premium writing the calls and at the same time get the benefits of holding the underlying stock such as dividends and voting rights. The profit potential in this strategy is limited since you have, in return for the premium, given up the chance to fully gain from a consequential rise in the value of the underlying asset.

Maximum Potential Profit

Besides the premium received for the entry to the call options, you will earn extra profit if the stock invested rises in value to the strike price of the call option. The maximum gain that can be achieved in this strategy can be calculated as shown below.

Max Profit = Premium Received (less) Purchase price of the underlying asset (add) Strike price of short call (less) commissions paid.

Maximum profit is attained when the price of the invested asset is equal to the cost of the short call.

Maximum Potential Loss

This strategy like any other has potential losses that are unlimited theoretically and occur when the price of the security drops. This risk however, can be mitigated by utilizing a stop loss in your stock trade.

Break-even

The break-even point for this strategy for the underlying price occurs and can be illustrated by the following formula.

Break-even point = Purchase price of the underlying securities (less) premium received.

This strategy is delicate and should be handled with care for beginners to succeed using it. You must take into consideration the downside before you commit your money into the trade.

d. Covered Puts Strategy

Covered puts are options strategy that involves writing put options as well as shorting the quantity of shares in the underlying asset. The graph below illustrates how the strategy works.

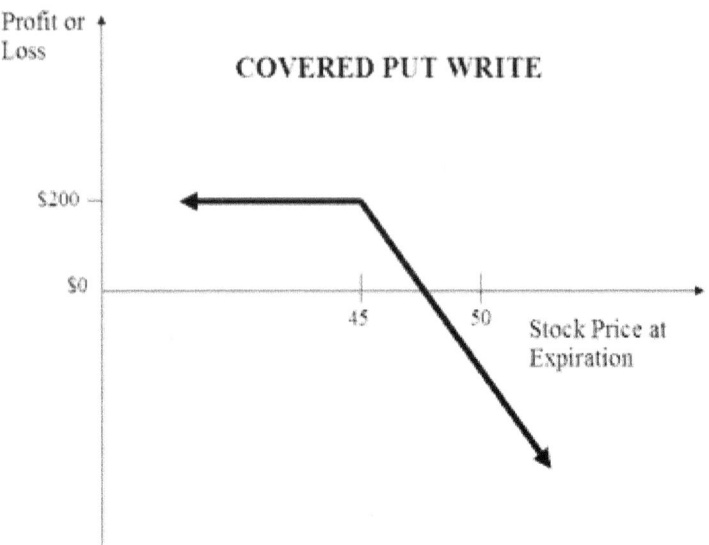

Maximum profit

The maximum profit that can be obtained using this strategy is dependent on the premium received for the sale of the options.

You can calculate the maximum profit that can be achieved in this type of strategy by the help of the formula below.

Maximum profit = Premium received (less) Commissions paid out.

The maximum profit is reached when the price of the underlying securities is equal to the price of the short put options.

Maximum Loss

Since you got to short the stock that is covering the put you are prone to a quantifiable amount of risk simply because the amount of risk could increase in value. To mitigate this potential cause of loss you are encouraged to use a stop loss on your options trade. However, there still exists significant risks that arise when using this strategy. It is advisable to ensure that you are well conversant with the risks involved using the formulas for calculating the potential loss of options trading as indicated below.

Loss = Price of the underlying securities (less) Selling price of the underlying securities (add) Premiums received (add) Commissions paid

It is also paramount to note that loss occurs when the price of the underlying stock is greater or equal to the sum of the premiums received and the sale of the underlying assets.

Break-even

The underlying price where break-even point is reached can be calculated using the following formula.

Break-even Point = Premium received (add) sale of underlying security.

Conclusion

This strategy is a significant one to learn and should naturally be included in your armoury if your wish is to succeed in trading of financial instruments. But you should be cautious since this strategy is for the brave. You are prone to many risks that may destroy your investments therefore you should have considerable care and the use of stop losses in the options trade using this strategy. For this reason, I recommend that you should first get more experience in virtual environments before you can commit real capital.

e. Long Strangle Options Strategy

As a trader, there are many strategies. Among them is the long strangle strategy where you buy a slightly out of money put and call for the same stock with the same dates of expiry. When using this strategy profit and risk are unlimited. It is applicable when you hope that the price of the assets invested will become volatile in the near future. It is a type of debit spread as it requires you to take a net debit to trade.

Maximum Profit

You can reap a lot of profits from this strategy if the stock prices fluctuate vastly before the expiry date. Regardless of the movement of the prices you will still profit. Therefore, to calculate this profit, the formula that can be applied is as shown below.

Maximum Profit = Price of the underlying asset (less) Strike price of the long call (less) Premiums paid.

Maximum Loss

When the cost of the underlying stock falls between the strike price of the options, then traders end up making losses. At this price, the options will expire worthless, and the trader will lose the capital required to enter the trade. The formula used to calculate the maximum loss is shown below.

Maximum loss = Net premium paid (less) Commissions Paid

It is also significant to consider that maximum loss happens when the price of the stock falls between the strike price of the long put and the long call.

Break-even

This strategy has two break-even points namely; the upper and the lower. The two points can be reached by solving the two formulas below.

Upper Break-even = Net Premium Paid (add) Strike Price of Long Call

Lower Break-even = Net Premium Paid (less) Strike Price of Long Put

Conclusion on the strategy

As a beginner you should not venture into this strategy since it is complicated. However, it is easier than many other options though. Experience and time in the market are virtues required to successfully benefit from this strategy. Again, through the utilization of virtual trading platforms to test out on theories will help a lot to see the best ways that can make you reap good profits.

Chapter 4. Tips for Successful Options Trading

Have you ever pondered in your brain why people do so well in the various tasks they do unlike others? Well, options trading is not different; it is just like any other money making business. Why is it that certain traders perform well regardless of the market woes? These option traders stand out because of certain traits that should be adopted by amateurs to reap success in the end. The tips are as highlighted below.

a. Sufficient Capital

The mistake which is common to new traders make is to invest a little capital expecting to multiply their stake exponentially and before long they are left with nothing. Investing enough money reduces the "hunger" to get rich quick and enhances more mature moves when trading. You as a beginner should, therefore, be careful especially on leverage option trading offers so that your capital is not wiped out.

b. Low tolerance for risk

One quality that successful traders have is their low tolerance for risk. To be in the market forever, you need to trade on assets that are less risky but highly rewarding. The concept is to ensure that the odds are always on your side as far as possible.

c. Trade only when there is an opportunity in the market.

Patience is a virtue; we all know that. Well, the patience I am referring to here is the need for a trader to have that self-discipline and wait for the right opportunity to knock. These opportunities should have all the odds skewed to the trades favour. Like a good trader you should be willing to wait until the right opportunity presents itself. Do not be enticed by the green and red numbers in the screen and end up investing everything thinking that you are missing out on something yet you are inviting losses. It is also important to know the cycles in the market as published in the Business Daily. Understanding the cycles provide the room to figure out which trades to invest and which ones to avoid.

d. Trading Plan

Before registering an account you should have a trading plan. It should not be in your head but it should rather be written down purposely for references. It looks more like a reality when something is on paper rather than in thoughts. This is crucial to your success as a trader of options.

e. Risk Management Plan

Don't risk money on what you cannot afford to lose. Be defensive on your trade always thinking about the worst-case scenario. Beginners however, are troubled since they do not understand what level of risk is implied by a trade. To counter this, it is important for beginners to split up the capital in order to share the risk. This way, regardless of what happens, you are not going to run out of capital. It is, therefore, crucial that a plan on which risks to venture in be documented before the entry to the options trading to facilitate the monitoring of risk levels. Since everyone ones to reap big from any business, as an options trader, ask yourself, what risk management norms have I put in place?

f. Control Emotions

Options trading is a journey and like any other, there are bends, uphill and downhill. This means at times you reap big while other times you lose. This requires some balance of emotions so that one may not quit the trade. This is because at times you lose on trades that you were 90% sure that it would turn out okay. This is why you should be guided by your trading rules no matter what.

g. Discipline

To be successful in options trading, one needs to have high levels of self-discipline. Beginners may find it difficult to exercise this and wait for the perfect opportunity to come. Therefore, one should not trade to in a view of eradicating boredom or due to excitement. It is recommended that you be rigid to your trading plan at all costs and avoiding trading strategies that you are not well conversant with.

h. Focus

Beginners tend to get carried away by the profit and loss numbers in their accounts. Keeping your head level is necessary. Know our goals, trading strategies and rules. Don't try to copy someone else or if you feel so distracted take a break from the trade for a while. Sometimes, withdrawing from a task is the best medicine that allows you to rejuvenate you thoughts and have a clean mind with focus.

i. Commitment

Trading in options requires a lot of commitment. Money is earned at a risk and thus you should spend all of your time to minimize this risk. You need to be conversant with the current trends in the market as well as market cycles. Look for online material to boost your knowledge on options.

Chapter 5. Risk Management Tips for Option Traders

Everybody wants to reap big from what they do. However, as a fact in life, only those who take an extra step are the ones who benefit more. We have to accept that there exists both winning and losing streaks.

Risk management is the process of reducing risk. We all have to be good risk managers to survive in the options trading market. There are many principles of risk management with the easiest being size positions correctly. It means that you should only trade a considerable number of contracts that will allow the going concern of your account.

It is tempting to increase your trades and thus self-discipline to minimize the risk is essential. You should clearly understand the risk and reward factor in the risk management plan. There are a number of factors to become a risk manager, but bear in mind that even though you might be making money, paying necessary attention to the risk involved is also your job.

Conclusion

Options trading is an interesting subject but to beginners may seem a very complex subject. To succeed, it requires a lot of perseverance, commitment, focus and sheer determination to achieve. The options business operates on uncertainties and thus requires a significant level of experience to make good profits. As a beginner therefore, it is highly recommended that you should stay close to successful traders as a way of learning through apprenticeship.

Thank You Page

I want to personally thank you for reading my book. I hope you found information in this book useful and I would be very grateful if you could leave your honest review about this book. I certainly want to thank you in advance for doing this.

If you have the time, you can check my other books too.

www.ingramcontent.com/pod-product-compliance
Lightning Source LLC
LaVergne TN
LVHW021744060526
838200LV00052B/3471